MW01235027

TREASURES
of the
HEART

by
Melinda Blair

Treasures of the Heart
by Melinda Blair

Printed in the United States of America

ISBN 9781628711950

www.xulonpress.com

TABLE OF CONTENTS

Chapter 1

TREASURES OF THE HEART

W hat is a treasure? Some people may view treasures as accumulations of worldly wealth. However, they may not realize that those possessions are just temporary; in order to find true treasure, they must seek with their hearts and collect the eternal ones, which are freely supplied by God. In Matthew 6:19, we are instructed to store up our treasures in Heaven, rather than waste our time gathering those that robbers and moths hunger for. When we take the time to really observe nature, seeing God's detailed patterns in butterfly wings, sunsets, sunrises, refreshing, gentle breezes on our faces and rainbows after the rain, we can almost hear a whispered *"I love you"* from God.

During the past few years, I have become addicted to seeking, gathering and sharing the special touches that God selectively sprinkles throughout my day. These "kisses from God" come in various forms and fashions, and each one is a beautiful reminder of His unconditional love. Some of them are tangible while others are not, but I cherish each one and add it to my daily collection. It has become a habit for me to thank God the very moment that I notice one. Many nights, at bedtime, I am amazed at the number of times He has touched my life. On those days when I am filled to overflowing, the lid to my treasure box won't even close!

"Treasures of the Heart" is a compilation of some of those special touches from God. Each of the photos and messages was completely presented and inspired by Him, and many of them are illustrated through His magnificent creation. Shortly after He gave me my first photo, I began sharing it with many people, and it turned into what I call my picture ministry. God steadily increased His provision of these unique gifts, and it has certainly generated a more personal walk with my Shepherd.

I will never forget the day when my heart was absolutely breaking, as God sent a butterfly to me. Because one of my nicknames is Little Butterfly, I now look at these small creatures with a new perspective. That butterfly remained close to me for over an hour. The memories of that day still tenderly touch my heart each time I look at the photos of the butterfly, as it crawled on my hands and up and down my arms. One of my favorite pictures is the one taken when I raised it with my fingertip to touch its wing to my nose. I will always remember that incredible afternoon, when I sat in the grass and simply soaked in God's love. My special visitor, with orange and black wings, was God's way of saying to me, *"I care, and I am here."*

We can easily add a little sparkle to the lives of others around us by simply giving a warm smile and a "Hello" to someone in our daily path. We are given many opportunities to help make someone's day a little brighter during our day-to-day routines in the workplace, and on the paths where our "to-do" lists carry us. People might not remember our names, but they won't forget how we make them feel. It doesn't take but a minute to smile and speak to employees who may not receive much recognition, and thank them for working hard. Just try it! If they are not already smiling, they will be by the time you leave and a compliment could add a beautiful ray of "SON-shine." On a hot summer day, surprising the mail carriers or the garbage collectors with a cold drink may seem rather small to us, but to them, it is big. Often times, the gifts that are the most meaningful are the ones that have little or no monetary value, especially when given to a stranger that you will probably never see again. Second Corinthians 9:6 tells us that if we sow generously, we will reap generously. There are so many people in the world who are hungry for love, hope, peace and joy; but the only kind that is everlasting comes from God. If we are willing to listen and respond, God will certainly place soft whispers in our hearts when someone in the path of our daily walk needs a little extra touch of His love, compassion and kindness. Personally, I like to think of such times as indoor rainbows, and Jesus uses them to add vibrant color to our days. He is the treasure at both ends of the rainbow.

I will always remember the special season in my life when I developed the desire for an intimate relationship with Jesus. As the relationship grew, He became my personal Shepherd and I began noticing signs of His love all around me. Those love notes from Him were scattered long before then, but I was not looking and listening. A heart is the universal sign for love, and I truly believe that is why I find so many of them strategically placed along my way. Hearts are prominent findings in my photo collection, and I perceive them as reminders of God's incredible love. I have found them in the sky, on trees, on the ground, in rocks, in food and just about any other place one can imagine. I am currently filling a second photo album. God touches our lives with things that touch our passions. Because they are so personal, there is not a doubt that they are gifts from Him.

For many years, I was not focused on God and had become a bit hopeless. Now I thank Him for those painful struggles and trials; for without them, I might not have run as fast as I could to Him. I would have missed out on the magnitude of His blessings. Anything that causes us to run faster to the Shepherd and love

Him more is worth every tear and heartache that it brings. By viewing life as the ultimate treasure hunt, we allow our hearts to become the treasure chest, and whatever is stored within will be the only wealth we can take with us when our life comes to an end. It has been proven to me that the more we gather to share, the more we will receive. That is a promise! So, enjoy the journey!

Chapter 2

THE SON SHINES BRIGHTER

One fall morning several years ago, I was sitting in my car in the parking lot of my church. I would not go inside the church because I was listening to some of satan's lies, and I just couldn't make myself go through the church doors. It was a chilly morning, but the sun was warming me as its beautiful rays were beaming through the car windows. God spoke something very powerful to my heart that morning, and He used the naked tree branches to convey His message. He showed me that the "SON" shines the brightest when we are empty. I was able to see more of the sun coming through the bare tree branches than I would have seen if the limbs had been covered with leaves. God's peace, love, comfort, hope and strength are always stronger when we are weakened by trials and struggles. The enemy is a loser and a liar, and I intentionally spell his name with a lowercase letter, because he deserves no honor!

Chapter 3

WORDS *DO* HURT

he old childhood chant about "sticks and stones may break my bones, but words will never hurt me" holds about as much truth as the enemy does. It holds none! Words "do" hurt and some of those wounds can leave huge holes in our heart…like wells dug to the deepest parts of our souls. These heart-shaped leaves, damaged by hungry bugs, represent the holes that are left in the hearts of people whose lives have been beaten down by poor choices of words. Physical harm is tough enough, but so often the words of mental and emotional abuse, slander and gossip can cut the deepest. They can also bleed the longest and may become the hardest to heal. Proverbs 18:21 tells us that life and death are in the power of the tongue: therefore, we must carefully choose our words. When nails are driven into a fence, they can be removed, but the holes still remain until they are patched. Psalm 23:3 promises us that the Shepherd restores our souls, and the fact that the God of the entire universe is our personal Shepherd gives us, as Christians, the hope of complete healing. He is the only One who can ultimately restore our souls and repair the holes in our hearts!

great host
and shall be

harpers, and
and trumpet
ore 1 Isa

raftsm...
all h...ound
e ...nd of a
more

candle ...mall
...ee; and ...the
...nd 1 Isa 8: 8
no   2 Nah
     Rev 17...

y merchants
e earth; 2for
all nations

he blood of
d of all that
a Jer 51:49

I heard a
people in
1 Rev 4:11:
7:10
...our, and
...his

The Word of God. S... bound
8 And 1to h... ...d that she
should be ...fine linen,
...or the fine 1 Ps 45:13
linen is the righteousness of saints. 2 Ps 132:9
9 And he saith unto me, 1Write,
Blessed *are* they which are called unto
the marriage supper of the 1 Lk 14:1
Lamb. And he saith unto me, Thes...
...re the true sayings of God.
...0 And 1I fell at his feet to worshi...
hi... And he said unto me, 2See *tho*...
do 1... not: I am thy fellowser- 1 Rev 22:
va..., and of thy brethren 2 Ac 10:
3... 3 1Jn 5
...at have the testimony of Jesu...
worship God: for the testimony
Jesus is the spirit of prophecy.

11 And I saw heaven opened, a...
behold a white horse; and he t...
sat upon him *was* called 1Faith- 1 Jn 1
ful and True, and 2in right- Rev
eousness he doth judge and m... 2 Isa
war.

12 His eyes *were* as a flame of...
and on his head *were* many cro...
and 1he had a name written, 1 Isa
that no man knew, but he him...

13 1And he *was* clothed with a ve...
dipped in blood: and his nan...
called 2The Word of God. 1 Isa 6
2 Jn

14 And the armies *which* we...
...llowed him upon

Chapter 4

TIE THE KNOT WITH JESUS

One night, while having my pillow prayer time, I received a message in the quietness of the moment. It was an extension to the old adage that says, "When you reach the end of your rope, tie a knot and hang on." God reminded me that Christians are the Bride of Christ. Therefore, if we tie the knot with Jesus, He will not (knot) forsake us: He will not break His promises to us; He will not fail in helping us fulfill His purpose for our lives and we do not have to fear what man can do to us!

The gold wedding band forms a heart-shaped shadow in the seam of the Bible, and it symbolizes the never-ending, perfect love of Jesus. His love surpasses all understanding. It is immeasurable, it is indescribable and it is the reason that He went to the old rugged cross. What a commitment!

Chapter 5

THE SON SHINES THROUGH

One day, while I was taking a walk through my backyard, I noticed this white mass on a pine tree. As usual, I had my camera so I began taking a few photos of the spider web that had almost overtaken the young tree branch. It wasn't until the sun peered out from behind a moving cloud that I was able to see all the bugs and debris that had become trapped in the massive webbing. There were many more insects and segments of leaves in the tangled fibers than I had first realized. It was then that the message God was showing me became very clear.

Until Jesus, the SON, shines His light into our hearts, we are sometimes unable to see the ugly debris, better known as sin that has become entrapped in our lives. God will tenderly, yet powerfully, give us the strength needed to release those things in our lives that hinder our intimate relationships with Him!

Chapter 6

THE LORD IS MY SHEPHERD

This is the way our Holy Shepherd holds us in His loving arms. Isaiah 40:11 tells us that He carries us in His arms and holds us close to His heart. Surround yourself daily with the kind of love, peace, joy, comfort, hope and strength that can only come from Jesus. The Shepherd desires only the best for us and cares for us more than we could ever imagine. Because of His unconditional love for us, He takes care of even the smallest detail.

This is why I want to always remain within arms' reach of the Shepherd and strive to walk in the shadows of His footsteps. Sheep are so lost without a shepherd, and we are "nothing" without Jesus in our lives. He will never turn His back on us, and those hands that we scarred will always pick us up.

When we surrender our lives to Jesus and ask for His forgiveness, we will no longer have to live in bondage. Our past will no longer cast a shadow on our future, and all our needs will be met. Life without Jesus is hopeless! (Psalm 23)

Chapter 7

WHAT MATTERS TO US
MATTERS TO HIM

These crosses are the focal points of an outdoor chapel at a local park and are located at the foot of several rows of elevated seating. A couple of years ago, I was there for a friend's candlelight service, and it was my first time to visit the camp. The camp is located on a lake and is quite a lengthy drive from my home, but I had really wanted to attend the highlight of the weekend's events. Several of my friends from my church had also planned to attend, and I knew in my heart that it would not be possible for me to go unless I was invited to ride with them. Because I did not feel comfortable inviting myself, no one was aware of my desire to go; but God knew it, and He took care of it.

A close friend from another church was driving back from her daughter's house that afternoon when she called me on her cellphone. She asked me if I would like to go with her to the candlelight service. As she began telling me how God spoke to her heart during her drive, tears filled my eyes. I was actually vacuuming when the phone rang, and I became saturated with excitement when I explained to her how God had used her as an angel. When we arrived at the camp, she asked me if I would like to walk down to the lake with her so she could show me the crosses.

The sunset was absolutely gorgeous!! Instantly, I reached into my purse for my camera; even though I knew the batteries were extremely weak, I tried to capture that moment in a photo. The camera would turn on, but kept shutting down each time I tried to take a picture. So I began praying that God would make it possible for me to get a picture of the sunset behind the crosses. I asked for "a" photo, but He gave me four! Wow! Since then, I have been given many opportunities to share this story and numerous copies of the photos. God planned the entire event and He certainly made it happen!

"In thy presence is fullness of joy: at the right hand there are pleasures for evermore" (Psalm 16:11). God enjoys adding special touches to our lives, and I have witnessed it many times and have no doubt of many more to come. This is why I believe that what matters to us, matters to Him!

Chapter 8

TURNING WINTER INTO SPRING

*W*hen I first saw these dead leaves continuing to hang on the branches of this tree, I thought about how it relates to our lives. God is the only one who can turn winter into spring, and He allows seasons in our lives to strengthen us and to mold us into what He has perfectly planned for our journey. The dead leaves that are still clinging to the branches symbolize those things in our lives that we need to let go of: bitterness, hate, resentment and guilt! The new growth that comes with springtime will gently push the dead leaves from the tree. If we choose to surrender everything to God and allow Him to turn the winter in our hearts to spring, then the Holy Spirit can replace those things with strength, beauty and the fruit of the Spirit!!

Chapter 9

THE HANDS AND FEET OF JESUS

When I notice trees with no signs of life, I am reminded of times when I have been surrounded by people, but still felt alone and empty. Just like the trees that are filled with an abundance of green leaves, we can become so full of ourselves and concerned about our own issues that we may fail to notice the pain and emptiness in the lives of others around us. In this life, we will experience trials and struggles, and some of the toughest ones may even cause us to quickly become hopeless or really discouraged. We may not truly realize how inspiring just a few words of hope or a warm smile can be for someone, or how much encouragement we can give by simply offering a loving heart and a listening ear. One of our daily prayers should be that we will hear the prompting of Jesus as He whispers to our hearts that someone around us is hurting and needs an extra touch from Him. May we always strive to be the hands and feet of Jesus to a hurting world!!

Chapter 10

TRAILS THAT SPARKLE

n the spring, one of my students and I were walking outside, and I noticed numerous "snail trails" along the edge of the sidewalk. The clover was in full bloom and the long stems had grown over the side of the walkway. The rich, green leaves were glistening because of the thin layer of morning dew, but the sparkle of the trails was even more obvious. The sun was causing them to shimmer like curly strands made from diamond dust. It made me question my own life. What kind of trails do I leave behind on the roads that I choose to travel and in the lives of the people that God places in my path? If we allow the "SON-shine" of Jesus to radiate from our hearts, we can leave trails that will sparkle and have meaning! We are given one life to live in this world, and we must choose to live each day to the fullest and to make the most of each moment while we still have breath!!

Chapter 11

THE LIFESPAN OF A BUTTERFLY

The average lifespan of a butterfly is approximately twenty to forty days. That is not a long time to fulfill their purpose in this life. However, during this time, they add so much extra beauty, vibrant colors and tender touches to our world. Their dancing and fluttering bring joy. We have no way of knowing just how long we will have in this life to fulfill our purpose. That is why it is so important for us to do no less than our best to carry out the unique plans God has for us, and to add beauty and pleasure to the lives of others while we can.

Chapter 12

THE BEST GIFT EVER GIVEN

The cross… a gift like none other! No other kind of gift could ever come close in comparison. Crosses in the sky made by jets remind me of the magnitude of Jesus' love. One day during the Christmas season, I was driving my car into town in hopes of completing my shopping. While parking the car, I noticed a white cross in the sky. I began hoping that others who were rushing to get the "right gift" would also notice it and be reminded that Jesus is the reason for the season. It was beautiful! The best gift ever given was not wrapped in a pretty package with a bow, but was wrapped in swaddling clothes and placed in a manger. Thank you, God, for your ultimate gift! (John 3:16-18; Romans 6:23)

Chapter 13

KISSES FROM GOD

Not all kisses from God come in butterfly form, but He will touch our lives with special things that touch our passions. Because each one is so personal, there will be no doubt that they are from Him. When we gather and share the kisses He gives, He continues to give us many more. God has a strong desire to have an intimate relationship with us, and He speaks to us throughout our day.

This butterfly was sent to me on a day when my heart was very heavy, and I was in need of an extra touch from God. My eyes were blinded with tears: therefore, I was unable to see God's hand in the issue I was facing. Because I am fond of butterflies, God used one to capture my attention. The Monarch butterfly remained close to me for a long time. Even after two quick trips inside my home, it came back to me when I returned outdoors. Butterfly visits do not usually last for a long time, so I knew that it was a representation of love and comfort from the Holy Spirit.

The issue that caused my heart to be sad was an unexpected transition in my job location, but God knew exactly where I needed to be. I am extremely happy in the placement He chose for me. A smile comes to my face each time I view the photos made on that "special touch from God" kind of day. God never fails to present His love and provision for us!

Chapter 14

REST IN HIM

These two ant bed photos were taken over a two day period, and the message within was also presented in that same time frame. I first noticed the ant bed early one school morning when I was walking through the parking lot, because it was just inches from the curb. Making photos of an ant bed is not something that I would have planned, but this one looked like a heart and it instantly captured my attention. God uses the most unique things in my path to reveal messages, and it is exciting to observe how He works. I quickly made a few photos before entering the school, and it's a good thing that it happened like that. About an hour later, one of the school's maintenance crewmen came to repair our air conditioner and his truck tires completely flattened the mound of red dirt. Even though the tiny ants had nearly completed their home, they wasted no time in starting the rebuilding process.

Out of curiosity, I kept checking on their progress to see if just maybe it would be another heart-shaped home. By late afternoon, I could see that the height of the mound was about half of its previous level, and I could hardly wait until the next morning to see the result of their all- night's labor. Early the next day, I found it to be a perfect circle and in that moment, I received the rest of the message.

The enemy tries so hard to tear us down, but if we have Jesus in our hearts, He will help us to be victorious in anything the enemy uses in his efforts to destroy us. We can certainly learn by observing little ants in their determination, but we do not have to work all night…we simply give it to Jesus and trust Him to repair any kind of brokenness and renew our minds! At bedtime, we can crawl up in the Shepherd's lap and rest in peace.

Jesus has a perfect balance of strength and tenderness, and His provision of each is also in His perfect timing. He was a Jewish carpenter, and He is a pro at rebuilding broken hearts and dreams if we allow Him to be the cornerstone in our lives. He is astonishing and I know He will be working on me until the day He returns. I like that! (Proverbs 6:6; 30:25)

Chapter 15

JESUS IS THE ROCK

When a rock is tossed into to the water, a ripple effect occurs. The same holds true in our lives when something is suddenly tossed into our daily routine or alters our dreams for the future. Our reaction in any situation will either hinder or raise our level of integrity and improve our character. Many times, the choices we make not only affect our own life, but can also affect the lives of the people around us. A rock causes ripples, and Jesus *is* the rock! A heart that is filled with Jesus can easily form positive and very meaningful ripples. It is our choice!

Chapter 16

SEEK HIM WITH OUR HEART

We can see Jesus through any dark and stormy cloud in our lives, if we seek Him with our hearts. In those times when our vision is blurred by tears, we have no other choice but to look for Him with our hearts. I see so many hearts in many different places, and I always know that they are from God. He leaves us little signs of His love all around us. This pale blue heart in the middle of this cloud reminds me of His ever-present love and His promise to carry us through the storms of life. God is able to turn our ashes into beauty and if we continue to trust Him, we will reap the rewards and have an abundant life!

Chapter 17

SEEDS OF HOPE

This baby pine tree was growing on the windowsill of an old building that was in the process of being torn down. The roof had already been removed, so the blue sky became visible through the open window. Not only does the blue add beauty to the photo, but it represents a clean slate on a new day. The metal windowsill was surrounded by mortar and it offered very little room for a layer of soil, but the pine seedling had just enough fertile ground to begin its growth.

Often times, after planting seeds of hope and inspiration in the hearts of those around us, an accumulation of months or even years may pass before we see any signs of harvest. Some of life's toughest struggles cause hearts to become bitter and hardened, and it may take much longer for germination to occur. Plant the seeds of hope anyway, because at some point in time, with God's help, those seeds will begin to sprout.

Many times when people travel through the deepest valleys and experience some of the darkest hours, they become desperate for God. As Christians, if we demonstrate stability, strength, peace and hope during the toughest of times, it may cause others to desire what they see in us. Sowing the seeds with sincerity and complete faith opens the door for God to do His part. He is the only one who can soften the hardened hearts and make them fertile enough to produce a bountiful harvest.

Chapter 18

HIDDEN BEAUTY

here is something very beautiful in everything that God makes. Sometimes that beauty is deeply hidden in certain situations, or even in the people who are a part of our lives. Because we are so accustomed to looking at things with our eyes, we will not see the hidden beauty, unless we look for it with our hearts!

Chapter 19

HEART-TO-HEART

This is a picture of a transmission tower that is one of many in a power company's right-of-way through a wooded area. A few days after this photo was made, I was in the midst of my evening pillow prayer time and received its message. Many times, during the quiet moments on my pillow when I am really listening for God's whispers, He gives me the words that relate to my photos. Sometimes He provides a message first, and I have no doubt that a photo is on its way.

The whisper that evening was about the heart shape made by the cross arms in the center of the tower. Very clearly, He showed me that until the hearts are connected, there will be no power. The long row of towers with hearts covers several miles through a cleared pathway in the woods. The power lines run from heart to heart to heart. Until the hearts are connected, there will be no power transmitted.

That's how our hearts are, too. God can use each of us every day to touch someone's life, and when our hearts are connected by Him....there is an amazing power! God shows His love to us every single day, but it is up to us to seek and cling to the strength He freely gives.

Chapter 20

CHAINS OF BONDAGE

This is a chain that I found near a wooded area. Even though I had previously seen it several times, it still scared me each time I glanced at it. Because it looked like a snake, I instantly thought about the story in the Bible when the enemy was disguised as a snake in the Garden of Eden.

The chains of lies, deceit, doubt, distortion and guilt are just a few of the weapons that the enemy tries to use against us. He tries to hold us captive, but he will never have a chain strong enough, or big enough, to withstand the magnitude of Jesus and all that He is in our life.

Jesus gave His life for us and rose again so that we may have an abundant life....a life filled with forgiveness, freedom, joy, hope, love, strength and complete peace. Jesus is so much bigger than anything we could ever face in our lifetime! (Galatians 5:1)

Chapter 21

DARE TO BE DIFFERENT

D are to be different! Even if you are the *only* one standing up for what is right….do it anyway. You are never alone! God will always be with you to provide strength and to help you live a life driven by strong integrity. This white Gerbera Daisy, with one purple petal, powerfully illustrated this message to me. What a beautiful remembrance of His love and His provision of ultimate strength!

Chapter 22

WAVES OF THE STORM

ate one night, while I was sitting on the floor beside my bed, the Holy Spirit delivered a powerful promise to my heart. Earlier during that day, one of my dearest friends had been a victim of a terrible incident, and it was absolutely breaking my heart. Because her pain was heavy on my heart, I refused to place my head on my pillow without a peace about the entire situation. Several hours passed as I searched in the Scriptures, read various pages in devotional books, listened to praise music, prayed and then listened for answers. I waited with expectancy. Sometime after midnight, I received the message and it was a promise for all those who believe.

The words that I received were, *"If your faith is stronger than the waves of the storm, you will not go under!"* I have continued to claim that promise, cling to it and will never let it go! Jesus has repetitively proven that to be true, because faith is a knowing that Jesus keeps His promises!

Chapter 23

GOD HOLDS OUR HEART

W hen our lives seem dark and stormy because of struggles and trials, we have the promise that God always holds our hearts in His hands. The white ring around the tiny blue heart at the top is a representation of the fact that He *is* the light in a dark world. God will never leave us alone in the darkness, and He will always have His hands outstretched to lead and direct us in the life plans that He has for us. Each and every day, He sends us little love notes that I call "kisses from God" to remind us of His love! We serve a mighty God! (Philippians 4:7, John 8:12)

Chapter 24

AN ANGEL WHEN WE NEED ONE

*W*e may not always get an angel when we ask for one, but we will always have one when we need one. Angels are sent for various reasons and in various forms, but they all share one characteristic.... they each come with a blanket of love, woven by Jesus. There is no kind of love that comes close in comparison to the love that Jesus freely gives!

Chapter 25

A HEART OF HOPE

Sometimes our hearts become frayed around the edges, and other times they break. The spider in this photo represents those things that we sometimes allow to creep into our hearts; things that can destroy us. Did you notice the brown "J" where the dirt was still moist in the middle of the heart? If we keep Jesus in the center of our hearts, the living water that can only come from Him can wash away those things that try to invade. It can heal the brokenness and repair the frayed edges. The green grass symbolizes life, even during our trials and struggles, because *nothing* is too big for Jesus to heal and restore. He is much bigger than anything we face in this life!

God can speak to us anywhere and anytime, if we are willing to look and listen.... even in the dirt. This heart picture was made in the bottom of a dried-up pond, and the spider crawled across it as I was making the picture. It was a very important part of the message. On the day this photo was taken, I had walked outside with my camera and was on a mission to find a special heart. After about an hour of looking and listening, God gave me this unique gift. He knew I would share it! (John 4:14)

Watch Your Step

ALABAMA
BUS SALES
866-621-7506
SALES • PARTS • SERVICE

Chapter 26

CHILD LIKE FAITH

A few days before this photo was made, I experienced a vision during a weekend nap. I had been sleeping for a couple of hours and even though I was trying to wake up, I continued to doze. I was awake enough to realize that I was having a dream, and I kept seeing the cross formed by the panels on the school bus doors. I assist students on a special needs school bus, and early last year, I noticed how the four panels of the door form a cross.

When I awoke from the dream, I knew that it was from God, because the Scripture about child-like faith was also a repetitive part of the dream. The words of the verse were familiar to me, but I didn't know where to find them in the Bible. I quickly began to search for it, and Mark 10:15 tells us that unless we have a child-like faith, we will not enter into Heaven.

Each day, young children enter our school bus as the cross of the doors open. They have complete trust and faith that we will care for them. Jesus' cross made the only way for us to spend eternity with Him in Heaven!

Chapter 27

WALK IN THE LIGHT

*A*nything that we allow to come between us and *"the SON"* will cause shadows and darkness in our lives. First John 1:5 tells us that God is light. Sometimes we allow things such as habits, jobs, pleasures or even other people to take dominance over our focus on Jesus. As a result, our priorities become off-balance, and we are no longer able to walk in the complete light that only He can supply. Oftentimes, lack of trust and faith can cause a path of darkness, because we have taken our eyes off the One who *is* light! Choose to walk in the light of the Lord as you seek His treasures, and extra sparkle will be added to your journey.

Chapter 28

DOUBLE PORTION OF LOVE

There is no way I could have completed this book without sharing photos of this heart shaped-rock. Late one winter afternoon, while driving home from an out-of-town appointment, I made a detour into one of my favorite places to have some "God and me" time. It is a special place on Lake Martin where I have captured many great photos, and the lighthouse, that is a focal point from the highway, adds striking beauty to the overall view. I have spent a great number of quality hours on the deck of the lighthouse, while praying and listening for God's voice. I think of those times as sitting at the feet of Jesus, because He is a light in the darkness and directs our steps.

The first half of the day had been overflowing with "wow" moments, and I knew that there had to be more on the way. If we wait with expectation, God shows Himself. I usually go visit the lake area when the water level is elevated but because it was during the winter, the shoreline was a bed of red clay with layers of rocks, dead leaves and sticks. As I stepped down from the bank toward the water, I said to God, "I know in all these thousands of rocks, there just has to be a heart rock somewhere. If there is one, please lead me to it." One can see in the photos that it happened.

After about twenty or thirty minutes of seeking, I found what I asked for in the foamy edge of the shoreline. My heart was already bursting with joy and amazement as I washed the mud from the top side of the rock, but when I turned it over, the excitement doubled. There was another heart on the bottom. One side of the rock is flat, and the other is a dimensional heart that looks like a folded paper valentine. I asked God for a heart rock and He gave me a double portion. He knew that I would show that wonderful gift to anyone and everyone. The more we praise Him and celebrate His goodness, the more He freely gives. To this day, I often kiss that rock and thank God for showing me, again, His extravagant love in such a personal manner. The rock is usually in the cup holder of my car, but sometimes it is in the bottom of my purse for those "need to share Jesus" times.

What is so amazing is that during those times, when God personally touches our lives, in the exact moment He is doing the same in the lives of people around the entire world. There is not one person in this world that He loves any more or any less. It is such a remarkably exciting way of life for me, now that I am living the life that Jesus died to give me. Even though I always ask with expectancy, His gifts still blow me away! Every time is as big as the first time!

Chapter 29

NEW LIFE IN CHRIST

*L*ate one afternoon, at the end of summer, I walked outside with my camera in hopes of capturing something for my book. As I toured the backyard near the edge of the woods, I noticed this little bug. Because of my newly developed love for nature, I made its picture. The orange-and-black colors, layered with the green background, made a pretty combination. Then, something that I had never seen before happened. Quickly after the first photo was taken, the bug sat up on its bottom side and I jokingly asked, "Are you posing for the camera?" I began making more and more photos, and within less than a minute, it began to shed its exoskeleton. As my observation continued, I became extremely excited about having the opportunity to capture such a wonderful presentation of God's creation on camera. The round body eased its way out the upper end, but it puzzled me. There were no spots. There was only a dull, pale yellow-colored body. It made its way to the right side of the empty skeleton and then after a few seconds, it crawled onto the top of the hollow, crusty skin. It did this two times before traveling to the opposite side of the leaf. At that moment, I was beginning to see the message within.

I lingered a while longer to see the rest of nature's beautiful display, but because it was nearing dusk, the woods were becoming darker. Even though the darkness made it difficult to see, I could tell that the outer layer of the new body was quickly becoming shiny and translucent. It had a wet appearance, and there were little black spots beginning to emerge as the yellow transformed into a more yellowish-orange color. My excitement grew stronger while watching the last phase of metamorphosis take place right before my eyes. As I waited and watched, the orange layer remained glossy as the black spots became much more obvious. It was an orange ladybug! I really wasn't sure until then, because I had never before seen a ladybug progress through the larvae and the pupa stages. New life had just begun!

This entire illustration of how perfectly God created every living thing in nature was a gift for me, and I will never forget that special afternoon. When I walked outside with my camera, I knew with all my heart that I would find something to capture during my treasure hunt, but never dreamed of anything such as this. Over the past few years, I have found that many lessons in life parallel with nature and, because I am a very visual person, each one leaves me with a lasting impression.

After the last photo was made, the entire message became as apparent as the little black spots. Just like the ladybug returning to its old skin, sometimes we lay our heavy loads at the foot of the cross, and then turn right back around and pick them up. When we completely surrender and trust Jesus with our burdens, He provides the strength required to leave them there. The ladybug traveled to the opposite side of the leaf to begin its new life. Getting rid of our old nature allows us to make a one-hundred-and-eighty degree turn and live in peace, as we begin our newly refreshed journey. God never ceases to amaze me, and my life's treasure hunt gives "thrilling" a whole new meaning!

(2 Corinthians 5:17) Therefore, if any man be in Christ, he is a new creature: old things are passed away; behold all things are new.

Chapter 30

THE DOGWOOD CROSSES

These dogwood crosses were made several years ago when I became really excited about Jesus and all that He is in my life. For many years, I would listen to people talk joyfully about their personal and intimate relationship with Jesus. Of course I would listen, but I didn't understand it because I lacked that in my own life. I now understand it and desire for everyone to have that kind of joy and excitement about Jesus. Sharing with others what Jesus does in your life may cause them to hunger for that kind of relationship! Make them want what you have!

The Bible does not specifically tell us what kind of wood was used for the old rugged cross, but dogwood blooms are a common symbol for Easter. The blooms add so much color and beauty to our world, and the cross made the only way for us to spend eternity with Jesus in Heaven.

Chapter 31

THE DESIRES OF OUR HEART

A few years ago, I became really interested in making photos of the sky. Most of them were pictures of sunsets and sunrises, but I also made some of the beautiful white clouds when they were thick and alive with bright light. After becoming so consumed with the relationship I have with Jesus as my Shepherd, I began to look and pray for a lamb cloud. I never saw one. Almost a year later, I was looking through some of my picture discs and as I was clicking from one photo to the next, I happened to see a cloud that looked like a lamb. It even had two ears and a nose. The first words from my lips were, "You already gave me one. Thank you God!" On the day this photo was taken, I was focusing on the fluffy white cloud between the blue canvas sky and the dark green trees. The moment I clicked onto this photo, I saw what I had been praying for. God knows the desires of our heart and fills our lives with His gifts. Isn't He amazing? (Psalm 37:4)

Chapter 32

SHARING THE LOAD

Any kind of heavy load in our lives becomes lighter when a friend shares that load, but God will carry that load if we will give it to Him. The best friends are those that God tenderly places in our lives, in His perfect timing and planning. These "Heaven-Sent" friends are cherished treasures, and they add lots of beauty to our lives. We don't travel this life alone, and we all experience days when we need a little extra dose of inspiration and words of encouragement. If we are listening and willing, God will use us to add extra touches of His love in the hearts of others, even if it is a stranger. He wants to fill our hearts until they overflow!

Chapter 33

OUR JESUS, OUR SHEPHERD AND OUR FRIEND

The Holy Shepherd will kiss our cheeks with whatever we need from Him. There may be times when we do not even know what to ask for, but He already knows exactly what we need. We can run to His arms and trust Him for complete rest and peace, because He is our Jesus, our Shepherd and our Friend. What more do we need?

CLOSING

A few years ago, when I became desperate for God, He began an exciting adventure for me and it has not dimmed in the least. When God presents me with the gift of a photo and then provides a message that corresponds, it always prompts finger kisses toward Heaven and a repetitive "Thank you God." Oftentimes, it's hard to keep my feet on the ground when He gives me one of those "wow" touches.

For instance, the photo of the morning glory leaves, damaged by bugs, has a unique story. The day before I made the picture, I had seen some heart-shaped leaves that were weak in color and damaged by hungry bugs. The bright, overhead sunlight hindered the quality of the photos, but I kept them anyway. Very early the following day, while I was getting ready for work, God began conveying the message to me. Later that morning, one of my non-verbal students was instrumental in God's provision for the beautiful photo. During our walk around campus, he indicated by pointing that he wanted to take the longer route. The vivid green leaves and the single pink bloom were on a vine that was clinging to the bricks on the backside of the building. There was not a doubt in my mind that God would provide a better picture, because He always gives us His best. I just had no idea that it would come so soon.

By now, I hope that you are convinced that God desires an intimate and personal relationship with each of us. Occasionally, I think about the years in the past when I failed to notice the special touches God planned for my days, but then I quickly direct my attention on the present-day time. The enemy knows that if we dwell on the past and the poor choices we have made, we cannot obtain complete focus and attention on our Lord. When we surrender ourselves to Jesus and trust Him for our salvation, it no longer matters what we have done. What truly matters is what He has done for us! Amazing Grace is no longer just a song on a page, but my style of living. It has caused me to realize that there are only two kinds of people in this world: those who are desperate for Jesus and those who do not know that they are desperate.

The enemy will try to tell us that Jesus cannot touch us where we are, and that our faith is hopeless in certain situations. That's when I tell satan that I did not ask him what he thinks and that I do not care. I have a slight speech impediment and sometimes before I share my testimony in front of a group, the enemy will tell me that I cannot get up and share because I stutter. That's when I tell him, "God knows how I talk, and He asked me to share, so I am doing it." Any kind of handicap, and we all have one of some sort, is only a handicap if we allow it to hinder what we are called to be. Do what you can. I have seen children with use of only one side of their bodies clapping with one hand to the rhythm of a song, but it was done with sparkle in their eyes and a smile on their faces. I love God's sense of humor. I once was an aide for a hearing-impaired student who read lips. Many days, she had to wait patiently when my words would get stuck.

For the past sixteen years, I have been an aide for children with special needs in the local public school system, and my dream is to continue for as long as possible. Over the years, I have assisted with children who were wheelchair-bound and non-verbal, but that did not keep them from leaving footprints in my heart and speaking to my spirit. I once told my principal that I figured out why our students were labeled special needs. It is because they meet many of "my" special needs. Some days, it is as if I can see Heaven through their eyes. Working with children with special needs has enlightened my outlook and altered my perception in certain situations. Life is exactly what we make of it, and the value within it is a reflection of how we look at things.

For an example, one cold and rainy morning, I was attempting to unlock the school door but was struggling because of trying to hold on to the oversized umbrella and tote bags. I kept dropping the keys, and it was hard to bend over to retrieve them. When I finally did get inside, I quickly said out loud to God, "I am O.K. I have a full tummy of oatmeal, a warm coat on my back, a key ring with a house key, a car key and a job key, and the wheelchair parked in the hallway is not mine." The enemy robbed me of so many years of joy, and I refuse to allow him to have another day of my life. Jesus gave the gift of joy to us, and it is not satan's to steal. He cannot take it in his own power. In order for him to obtain our joy, we have to grant it.

I am also a proud mother of two beautiful children, who are now grown, and I honestly believe that if God had given me the option of choosing my own children, I would have chosen the son and daughter that He has blessed me with. Jesus abides within their hearts, and He has enabled them to make wise choices. One thing that I emphasized to them was their need for good character and strong integrity. I repetitively told them, "Make choices today that you will be proud of in the morning."

When Jesus lives in our hearts, the past no longer has to cast a shadow on our futures. He will make a way when there is no way. Jesus is the *way maker,* and we could never do His job, because He does the impossible. The reassuring touch of the Shepherd's hand will suddenly bring light to the paths that trials try to darken. Giving our burdens to Jesus will provide us with complete freedom from bondage. He can handle them. He has a perfect balance of tenderness and strength, and His timing in the provision of each is also perfect. Some of my most cherished moments with the Shepherd are those times when I sit quietly and visualize myself as a little lamb in His arms. While taking long, deep breaths, I ask Him to hold me close to His heart (Isaiah 40:11). One of my daily prayers is that Jesus will cradle me so close to His chest that His heartbeat becomes "my" heartbeat. I also ask Him to overfill my heart with so many good things that it leaves no room for the ugly.

Beneath the headboard of my bed, I keep several stuffed prayer lambs to hold during pillow prayers. I especially like to choose one that best fits someone who is need of an urgent prayer. While praying for a male, I hold the one that has very long arms and legs, and I reach for a small one when I am praying for a child. My favorite lamb is also the softest and is the one that remains close to my side until the morning. Sometimes when I awake during the night, I will search for it and wrap my fingers around it. Doing so delivers layers of comfort that I embrace. In my personal opinion, the child-like spirit that I have is the source of motivation for my strong faith. The sheep's relationship to the shepherd is one of absolute dependence. It is one of protection, rescue and guidance. The Good Shepherd has invested too much in us for Him to ever turn away from us!

While looking for some previously written notes for use in this book, I ran across a letter that I had written last fall on the last day of the Labor Day weekend. The get-away weekend was an opportunity to spend alone time with God, and it gave me three days of complete focus and meditation. The letter is addressed to God, but I wanted it to be the closing of this book. My quiet times alone with God are some of my most valuable *"treasures of the heart!"*

Dear God,

e have lots of mountains to climb and miles to go, but You, my Shepherd, will be by my side every step of the way. Thank You for directing my path and when I fail to follow Your direction, please speak a little louder to confirm Your will for me. I want yours to be the only voice I hear. I continue to cling to the powerful promise that You gave to me one day while I was traveling on Highway 280. You told me that I will always be a target for satan, but will no longer be his victim! Even though for many years I was not focused on You and all that You want me to be in my life, You never took Your eyes off me and I was protected by You. The sad part is that I wasn't even aware that I was in need of protection and guidance. You have been, and You always will be, my rainbow of hope. You are the treasure at both ends! You keep me going both day and night and without You, life would be hopeless. With You, I can do anything, because You *are* my strength.

You never promised that life would be easy, and without trials and pain, but You did promise that I would never have to journey alone! The fact that there are many days with only one set of footprints in the sand does not reflect weakness on my part, but the contrary! Acknowledging that I am nothing without You demonstrates strong judgment and complete trust. The fact that I am nothing without You proves that *You are enough*! You have a perfect balance of tenderness and strength, and the timing of Your provision of each is also perfect and amazing. If my plans are not your plans, please make them crumble and fall apart.

I am praying for answers, and I am confident that You will provide all of them. The answers cannot come all at once, because all of the questions have not yet been asked. I cherish the fulfillment of Your promises and for meeting every need I have. My child-like faith is strongest during the deepest of struggles and the older I become, the stronger my faith develops. Thank You for always being just a breath away, and for loving me unconditionally. Your breath of hope is on my cheek. Sometimes when You hold me, it is as if I can feel your chest rise and fall upon my back. I love You and thank You for forgiving me for every failure and for every poor choice I have made. Thank You for being my Jesus, my Shepherd and my Friend!!!! My get-away weekend with You completely filled my heart with an abundance of comfort, hope, strength, peace, love and endurance. You are who You say You are, and that's all I need! I am, also, who You say that I am...someone worth dying for. What more could I ask for? I love you with all that I am.

CPSIA information can be obtained at www.ICGtesting.com
Printed in the USA
LVOW02*0050230514

387038LV00002B/3/P